ML   +
796.7 Sp18m
Spalding, Lee-Anne T.
Monster truck racing

MONSTER TRUCK RACING

The Thrill of Racing

LEE-ANNE T. SPALDING

Rourke
Publishing LLC
Vero Beach, Florida 32964

www.rourkepublishing.com

PHOTO CREDITS: © Ford Media: page 4, 17, 20 top; © Barry Salmons: page 6, 22 bottom; © felix casio: page 7, 11 ; © lori05871: page 8; © qds381chase: page 9; © Raigl: page 10; ©R. Gino Santa Maria: page 11 top; © JustASC: page 12; © Michael Stokes: page 13, 21; © Denise & Michael Vaters: page 15; © Maksim Shmeljov: page 19; © jurvetson: page 22 top;

Editor: Meg Greve

Cover and Interior design by: Tara Raymo

Library of Congress Cataloging-in-Publication Data

Spalding, Lee-Anne T.
  Monster truck racing / Lee-Anne T. Spalding.
     p. cm. -- (The thrill of racing)
  Includes index.
  ISBN 978-1-60472-373-1 (hardcover)
  ISBN 978-1-60472-810-1 (softcover)
  ISBN 978-1-60472-772-2 (ebook)
  1. Truck racing--Juvenile literature. 2. Monster trucks--Juvenile literature.
I. Title.
  GV1034.996.S73 2009
  796.7--dc22

                              2008011246

Rourke Publishing

www.rourkepublishing.com – rourke@rourkepublishing.com
Post Office Box 3328. Vero Beach. FL 32964

Table of Contents

When the Rumble Began

The roar! The rumble! The crushing! The applause! Monster trucks have been thrilling audiences for over 30 years. It all began with truck owners **lifting** their own trucks with lift kits and large tires. Bigfoot, the first true monster truck, **debuted** in the Pontiac Silverdome in 1982. This was the beginning of these popular car crushing events.

MANY MONSTER DEBUTS

1982	1999	2001	2005	2006	2007
Bigfoot, Black Stallion, Grave Digger	Madusa	Wolverine, Blue Thunder	Superman	Batman	Donkey Kong

Auto...Bio

Bob Chandler created Bigfoot. He originally stuck 48-inch (123-centimeter) tires on his Ford F250 and drove it over a row of junk cars. Since then, the Bigfoot **fleet** has grown to 17 Bigfoot monster trucks.

Monster trucks are built for racing and **exhibition** events. Up to 24 trucks race in groups of two at an event. These trucks also perform amazing stunts during freestyle events. Modern competition monster trucks have two very **distinctive** features: enormous 66-inch (168-centimeter) tires and flashy fiberglass bodies.

Thrilling Fact

The easiest way to get in and out of a monster truck is through a special **hatch** in the truck bed.

A Safe Ride

You can see a red light in each truck's cab which signifies that it is equipped with a remote **ignition** interrupter. If anything goes wrong during any portion of the event, a **crew** member can stop the truck with a remote control.

During a race, monster trucks get beat up. After each race, truck owners and crews must repair their vehicle. Common parts in need of repair are: fenders, paint, decals, headlights, and taillights. Tires often need replacing as well. It requires fifty hours to cut these tires by hand.

You Asked...

Can a monster truck legally drive on the road?

No! A monster truck measures 11 to 12 feet (3.35 to 3.66 meters) in width which is about three feet (1 meter) over the legal width for roads. Semi trucks or trailers haul them to each of the events.

In 1988, the Monster Truck Racing Association, or MTRA, formed to initiate rules for truck construction, performance, and safety. One safety rule requires all onboard fuel to be strapped down by a minimum of two metal straps. Another rule refers to ride trucks, or trucks that take audience members for a thunderous ride. These drivers and passengers must wear their seatbelts at all times and no dangerous maneuvers can be performed while passengers are onboard.

Caution: Danger Zone

According to the MTRA, to protect against fire, each truck must carry a fire extinguisher weighing at least two and a half pounds.

Monster truck fans have many choices when it comes to choosing a favorite truck. Many of the most popular trucks even have their own websites which provide information on the truck and its driver.

Grave Digger

Grave Digger and Bigfoot are huge **rivals**. In fact, this rivalry is one of the biggest in the sport of monster truck racing. Grave Digger is distinctive due to its many crashes and flashy paint job. The truck displays a graveyard scene with green flames and red highlights.

Bigfoot

You Asked...

Has Bigfoot ever been in a movie?

Yes! Bigfoot has appeared in eight movies.

Did you know that Bigfoot can reach speeds over 80 miles per hour (129 kilometers per hour)? Bigfoot's speed is fast, but building a Bigfoot can take from three months to one whole year.

Madusa

A female driver named Debi Miceli drives Madusa, a popular monster truck named after an ancient Greek mythological figure named Medusa. She was the very first female to drive a monster truck on the United States Hot Rod Association (USHRA) circuit.

Auto-Bio

Debi Miceli was born in Italy in 1963. At first, she was a professional wrestler. She retired from wrestling in 2001 to become a monster truck driver.

Black Stallion

Black Stallion is a monster truck named after the horse from the popular children's book and movie of the same name. For this reason, the truck's paint job is yellow and black resembling a horse's face.

Thrilling Fact

Black Stallion was the first monster truck to successfully jump another monster truck while driving in **reverse**.

Batman

Many monster trucks are designed after popular comic book characters, like Batman which debuted in 2006. Batman is a **replica** of the Batmobile, which is seen in comic books and movies.

You Asked...

What other monster trucks are named after Superheroes?
Spiderman, Sandman, Wolverine, and Incredible Hulk are superhero monster trucks, too!

Blue Thunder

The Ford Motor Company built Blue Thunder to advertise its "Ford Tough" truck. Blue Thunder competes in more than 20 events per year and has gained popularity with monster truck fans since its 2001 debut.

Big Events

Monster truck events or series take place all around North America and Europe. The Monster Jam series is the largest series with the greatest number of events offered year round. These events take place in many countries like Australia, Ireland, New Zealand, and Venezuela.

Where in the World Can You See a Monster Truck Event?

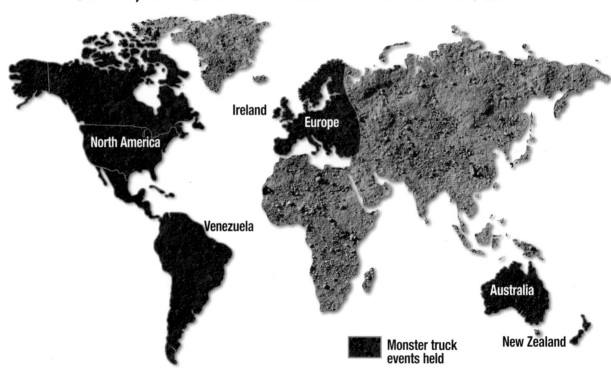

Ireland

Europe

North America

Venezuela

Australia

New Zealand

Monster truck events held

You Asked...

How much dirt is needed each year to create monster truck tracks?

700,000 cubic yards (535,188 cubic meters) of dirt is used each year in USHRA Monster Jam Events.

Thrilling Fact

You can visit the world record holder for the largest monster truck, Bigfoot #5, at the Home of Bigfoot store in St. Louis Missouri.

The average monster truck costs at least $150,000 to own and maintain. The large tires themselves cost about $2,600 each. When the race is over, repainting one monster truck can cost $3,500.

Thrilling Fact

Each monster truck racing team spends about $250,000 each year on repairs, racing uniforms, fuel, and travel expenses.

Monster truck racing and freestyle events continue to thrill audiences worldwide. Televised events and a huge number of fans have helped the sport grow. Each year about 3 million fans attend monster truck events in the United States alone.

Chances are, if one event has ended in your area, another one will return before you know it.

Glossary

crew (KROO): a team of people who work together on a specific job

debuted (day-BYOOD): appeared in public for the first time

distinctive (diss-TINGK-tiv): making a thing different from all others

exhibition (ek-suh-BISH-uhn): a public display

fleet (fleet): a group

hatch (hach): a covered hole in a floor, deck, door, wall, or ceiling

ignition (ig-NISH-uhn): electrical system of a vehicle that uses power from a battery to start the engine

lifting (LIFT-ing): raising something

replica (REP-luh-kuh): an exact copy of something

reverse (ri-VURSS): backward

rivals (RYE-vuhls): competitors

Index

Websites to Visit

www.allmonster.com

www.MonsterNationals.com

http://monsterphotos.com/

Further Reading

Harrison, Paul. *Monster Trucks (Up Close)*. PowerKids Press, 2008.

Mead, Sue. *Monster Trucks & Tractors*. Chelsea House Publications, 2005.

Poolos, J. *Wild About Monster Trucks (Wild Rides)*. PowerKids Press, 2007.

About the Author

Lee-Anne Trimble Spalding is a former public school educator and is currently instructing preservice teachers at the University of Central Florida. She lives in Oviedo, Florida with her husband, Brett and two sons, Graham and Gavin.